GRACE HAS
A SILENT VOICE

NINA M KELLY, PH.D.

BALBOA
PRESS

A DIVISION OF HAY HOUSE

Author Credits:
Myth Making and Modern Medicine, a case of Kidney Transplantation. The Lost Heritage, Psychology at the Threshold, and Saving Wednesday Child, forward and acknowledgement

Book Cover:
Barry James Cooper, Jr. Esq. photographer
Lawrence C Fothe, editor

Balboa Press books may be ordered through booksellers or by contacting:

Balboa Press
A Division of Hay House
1663 Liberty Drive
Bloomington, IN 47403
www.balboapress.com
1 (877) 407-4847

Print information available on the last page.

ISBN: 978-1-5043-2508-0 (sc)
ISBN: 978-1-5043-2510-3 (hc)
ISBN: 978-1-5043-2509-7 (e)

Library of Congress Control Number: 2014921905

Balboa Press rev. date: 2/27/2015

CONTENTS

FOREWORD

A story evokes our emotions and memories, including those quiet tears and the realization that we are connected to something so much bigger than the world we see around us. The story is an invocation of a time known by the author, who now shares the contours of his or her world with us. There are natural storytellers, those whose stories are as genuine as the author's heart and soul. Free of histrionics and unnecessary exaggerations, theirs are fed by the fires of sincerity and the need to make sense of the life that is theirs. It is because of this that we are inspired and moved by their words. Nina Kelly is such a teller of story.

In this series of letters written to a friend, Nina Kelly reminds us that resilience often lives side by side with grief, doubt, love, and joy. In one letter we are brought into the domain of the unimaginable wherein Nina has to tell a man that his wife and daughter were killed in a car accident. If that hell were not enough, she has to ask if he would agree to have their organs donated so that another could see the new dawn. In his acceptance, we can literally feel the presence of grace in life. As they are woven throughout this book, we see how life and death, as well as grace and tragedy, create the tapestry of life.

And then we read of a time when the muse arrived in the middle of a profoundly moving symphonic experience to tell her that a loved one would soon be gone. As a scribe recording the commandments from a high, she feverishly wrote every word and line that came to her during this visitation. Then the reality of what these muses wanted her to know came crashing down into her world as her beloved was suddenly found dead.

So words, invocation, and the power of what is in her heart allow us all to feel what it means to fully live in the world while imitating the much larger scope of living beyond the veil of all that is familiar a little more deeply and little more meaningfully.

And now there are the other letters in this book waiting to be opened. These letters are a gift to all of us on life's journey, reminding us of the native resilience alive in our souls. So with a cup of tea or glass of port, relax in your favorite chair while opening these letters. Smile and cry as you read about the escapades of a woman capable of turning planes around in midair, a woman who listens whenever possible to those voices alive within her soul that constantly bring her into relationship with the transcendent.

Dr. Michael Conforti
Founder of Assisi Institute, Jungian Analyst
Stonington, Ct.
September, 2014

Acknowledgment

In the winter of 2004 I wanted change. My life was fun. I had a great social life and an interesting job at a local museum. I didn't own a car and loved the smallness of my world. Nina had just become president of the Children's Bureau of New Orleans, and I thought that perhaps I could do some good in a volunteer role. Nina put me to work immediately in writing a history of the Children's Bureau of New Orleans, Louisiana. We shared a number of lunches together, talking about the project, and her enthusiasm really sparked something inside of me.

We made a lot of progress on the book together. We found each other again after Hurricane Katrina. The existence of the Children's Bureau, which had been around for over 114 years, was very much in doubt.

Nina was busy reconstructing the agency and securing the funding necessary for it to survive. She involved me with some of the early post Katrina meetings of the Children's Bureau staff held in Nina's apartment, and she directly tied the work that I was doing on the history of the organization to the effort to save the institution.

In May of 2006, she organized a fundraiser for the organization with a theme celebrating its history. The event featured music by renowned musician and composer Allen Toussaint and food prepared by New Orleans chef Leah Chase. The book itself, which was published in 2008, was used as a fundraising device for the Children's Bureau. Nina paid for the production of the book herself, and the revenue generated by sales were pumped back into the Children's Bureau.

Since taking that first step to contact Nina, my life has changed in many ways. I have published two more books and done things that I never thought I would do. My world is infinitely larger, and my sense of self-worth continues to grow.

Mark Cave, Senior Curator and Oral Historian, The Historic New Orleans Collection

Carol Lund

Preface Letter by Nina M Kelly, PhD

Dear Carol,

In writing these stories to you, it is my intention to express my thoughts concerning the voice of grace that speaks through so many lives. I am truly grateful to have seen and lived through such profound experiences. As you know, not all journeys in life are easy. Many of them we might wish had stopped on other doorsteps. But as I have spent time on this earth, I have come to realize that their visitation moves us toward the ultimate goal of gratitude.

The word *grace* has been used in numerous manners throughout history; individuals name their children Grace and even carry the surname. And we are apt in noting their character and mannerisms to compliment others' grace and style. However, the grace that I am addressing manifests in profound acts of kindness and charity offered as unconditional gifts.

Each of the following stories demonstrates that grace still lives today, as vibrant and unwavering as in the periods of ancient myth. The Greeks expressed belief in its power by introducing the three Graces whose purpose was to bring joy to the world and peace to the hearts of men. Daughters of Zeus and the Oceanid Eurynome, the three Graces were conceived as smiling divinities there to help people enjoy life and to ease social interaction. What a common occurrence for that ancient period, it was as natural as the use of our imagination today comforting us in times of need.

Grace expresses itself in another form as well. Musical grace notes are simple appoggiatura, little secondary notes performed as quickly as possible before an essential note in a melody. In my experience, such inconspicuous notes have sometimes been performed as a prelude to carry me from one chapter of life to another. Grace has come to me in music, with little or no knowledge on my part at the time of its visitation. The sound of music continues to grace my heart during moments of sadness, loneliness, joy, and celebration. I don't assume it confines itself to just one motif.

Then there is grace of spirit. This is the unconditional gift the universe presents to humankind each day. The gift of life and all it encompasses. I particularly enjoy the way Matthew Fox writes about the grace of nature in his book, *Natural Grace.* He speaks about nature and grace working together and how we humans are exposed daily to the grace of life and the beauty of nature in a remarkable array. Truly a gift we might acknowledge through gratitude.

Nature stands alone and each moment attempts to share richness with humanity. It offers itself with the hope that mortals will learn and return the favor. The grace of the Spirit of God speaks through such unconditional acts of kindness, whether delivered through nature or man. Wherever the heart is vulnerable, grace patiently waits to see if the gift will be welcomed.

As I relate these stories to you, I hope they communicate, in some manner, how grace flows into our hearts at critical periods in life and thus allows both the giver and the receiver the opportunity to give it full expression. In each of the stories, people rise to the occasion without hesitation. Subsequently, they offer this charitable gift of grace.

So my dear, sweet Carol, as always, thank you for allowing me to share these moments, memories that imprinted so deeply that they are never to be erased. They stay as perpetual reminders of the resilience of the human spirit and the heroic journeys on which we so often embark. These are profound visitations that will ever remain deeply embedded in my heart. I wonder if those individuals understood what a difference they made in the world. Grace in it's silence created a difference in the life of all who were willing to receive.

Always,
Nina

THE AUTHORS

Nina M. Kelly, PhD, is the author of *Grace Has a Silent Voice*. She has a doctorate in mythological studies with an emphasis on depth psychology. She did her dissertation, entitled *Myth Making and Modern Medicine, a case of kidney transplantation,* through Louisiana State University Medical School in New Orleans. Dr. Kelly also published the article, "The Lost Heritage, Psychology at the Threshold." Nina has worked in the medical field as a procurement and transplant coordinator nurse as well as private duty with death and dying patients. She has been a cultural activist for her community, holding numerous board positions as well as presidency for several associations. Dr. Kelly also served as the president and CEO for the Children's Bureau. She wrote the foreword and acknowledgement to *Saving Wednesday's Child.*

Currently, she holds the position of president for a newly formed foundation called SOFA (Academy of Creative Arts Shreveport, Louisiana). Her passion has always been for the overall improvement of humanity through the healing arts.

Dr. Michael Conforti is the founder of the Assisi Institute, Jungian Analyst, author, and film script consultant. He authored *Field, Form, and Fate, and Patterns in Mind, Nature and Psyche* and *Threshold Experiences: The Archetypes of Experiences.* Dr. Conforti lectures extensively throughout the United States and internationally. He has graciously agreed to write the preface of this book.

Mark Cave, senior curator and oral historian of The Historic New Orleans Collection, is author of *Saving Wednesday's Child,* the history of the Children's Bureau whose archives are housed at The Historic New Orleans Collection. He is also the author of *Listening on the Edge: Oral History in the Aftermath of Crisis,* and *Drawn to Life: Al Hirschfeld and the Theater of Tennessee Williams.* Mark has graciously agreed to write an acknowledgment.

Photography Acknowledgements:

Jackson Beals, Photographer, Nina M Kelly
Alex Zankevich, New Ground Photography, Carol Lund
Barry James Cooper, Jr., Esq. book cover and back cover
Morgan Nina Petersen, child
Nina M Kelly, PhD, photos

CHAPTER 1

TRAGEDY AND GIVING

Dear Carol,

We have been graced to live past our twenties and enjoy those first few years of a youthful marriage when the world was our dream. Not everyone gets that luxury. You and I have spoken of early times with our husbands and children, and that is the reason I want to share the following story. I wonder if I would have been as gracious as this husband?

In a very southern town in Louisiana lived a young, vibrant schoolteacher. She always thought her method and desire to make a difference in the young students' lives would someday be her legacy. Nancy was quick-witted and playful in her approach to teaching. She believed that if the children had fun while learning then all life's teachings would present different modes of inspiration. So she set her mission to stimulate the young minds of her students. This also encouraged her to be more creative in her methodology of teaching.

Each morning she looked forward to the eager young minds. She chose to position the little ones into a place in her heart. Nancy was a second-grade teacher, and she knew this was an important age for the little boys and girls. Her manner of instruction, discipline, and kindness were pivotal in their young lives. The self-assured qualities of these fresh little minds would hopefully leave an indelible print to guide them in their days ahead. Although she was in her early twenties, Nancy took her position most seriously. She knew teaching was her destiny and gift.

Early in her career, Nancy was not yet a mother herself and therefore gazed upon each of her students in a very tender and embracing light. She set her goal to being the best teacher for the second graders. She made up her mind to be a role model for these children. She did not know all of their personal stories, but she knew that while they were in her classroom she could offer them a school year of guidance on many fronts. Such had been the case for her. Her mother died when she was very young, and it was a second-grade teacher who had helped her through that terrible year.

Maybe that was why she decided to become a second-grade teacher. She had never told anyone except her family members how the smile and kindness of Miss Wallace helped her address each day without her beloved mother. The years passed quickly in her life. She always remembered Miss Wallace making such a lasting impression. Privately, maybe she knew that all the long and empty nights after her mother's death were somehow softened by the smile, gentle instruction, and teachings of that wonderful second-grade school teacher.

So Nancy inspired her little students daily. Without a doubt, she knew this was her true calling in life. Pleased to enter the classroom each day, a new story of her experiences with those talented young minds captured her husband's interest. He often found her stories amusing. He marveled at her patience because he knew he would never be suited for such a career. Can you imagine maintaining the attention of twenty-seven eight year old children? Such a thought sent shivers down his spine and inspired admiration for his beautiful bride.

Life carried on day to day with the normal routines, his career challenges, and her love of the classroom. Both were so busy, yet happy building their home and life together.

Then, as she drove to work one day, the unexpected happened. Crossing an intersection, a speeding car ran a red light and hit her car broadside. Once the ambulance arrived Nancy was rushed to the hospital and placed immediately on a ventilator. Having sustained severe head injuries, she was not able to breathe without the assistance. Lying helpless, she appeared so young and fragile. Her body still showed remnants of blood from the car accident. Nancy's head sustained such an acute trauma that she suffered massive cranial hemorrhaging. In the hospital bed her body lie still, to the untrained eye she appeared to be asleep. Nancy was never to regain consciousness. Her demeanor displayed the absence of movement, lifelessness. In an instant, life was stolen, dreams broken, a future robbed.

Once her husband arrived, he gazed upon his young, beautiful wife who had such incredible talents to share. Now everything had been taken from her. Speechless, he stared in disbelief. Memories raced through his mind as he recalled the morning and the tenderness his precious wife displayed walking out of the door. As he stood next to her and held her hand, he prayed for resolve of this horrific nightmare. The hours passed, and each hour seemed longer than the hour before. No change. Frozen in place and pale, he held her hand and hoped against hope for some response. No change came, just a lifeless hand.

"Wake up! Be strong!" he pleaded. Over and over he prayed for her to come back to him. Tears flowed from his eyes as he stood there in disbelief.

After twelve long and enduring hours, the worse nightmare happened. The door to her room opened, and the medical doctor slowly paced to the front of the bed and requested that Nancy's husband leave the room while he examined her neurologically.

Mark turned and removed himself from this surreal scene. Just prior to departing he turned and spent what seemed like eternity focusing on the image of his beloved wife. Still in shock from the morning's events, he moved slowly.

Impatiently waiting outside the door and listening carefully in case good news would arrive, Mark stood quietly. The hospital noise seemed amplified— moving carts, papers rattling, and buzzers going off from the adjacent patients' depleted IV medications. How much more would he need to endure before the doctor would give him word? The sound of the opening door announced the doctor leaving the room. Eye to eye, Dr. Roberts spoke in a quieted manner, causing Mark to strain to hear every word.

"We have just declared your wife brain dead," stated Dr. Roberts.

Dr. Roberts continued to speak, but all was silent to Mark. All he could hear was *brain dead*. He knew Nancy was gone and would not return to him. As the doctor spoke and tried to explain everything to him, nothing made sense. He knew what the term brain dead meant, he knew that she was physically dead and soon the respirator would be removed and this precious person would cease to exist. How could this happen? She looked radiant in the bed.

Reentering the hospital room and moving toward her, he held her hand with such tenderness as deep compassion embraced his heart. Nothing else mattered except these last moments together. How would he recover from this void? They had just begun their life together. This was not fair. The entire situation was out of his grasp.

"Don't let this happen. Don't let her leave. She has so much to offer this world." All these thoughts continued to flow faster than he could comprehend.

And then, when he thought he could not handle another decision, the door once again opened to another stranger entering.

I introduced myself as the procurement coordinator from the medical school. He did not know what that meant. Expressing my compassion for his loss, I continued to explain the term brain death. Still stunned, he could not move. My position was to ask consent for organ donation. This was never an easy task. It was difficult to approach a loved one at the time of death and request consent for donation.

Nancy had signed her driver's license stating she wanted to be an organ donor if possible, and had even discussed this with her husband. Little did either one of them know that this request would come so early in her life.

However, in the case of vascular donors, time is critical. I left the room to allow Nancy's husband to spend the time he needed with his beloved.

After several hours he requested that I return. He'd decided to donate her vascular organs and tissue to allow others the opportunity to live. It is most difficult having to face that your wife will never return home, to her classroom, or to her family. His anguish cut to the core of his being. He thought this could not be happening as their life together rushed through his mind.

A gift of life cannot be measured. As he focused on his lifeless wife, he knew she would never be able to share those precious, amusing stories over breakfast again. Someone else would have a chance to live. Nothing was making sense in all of this despair. Yet time and time again, the human heart opens up to the gift of life, grasping to make some sense of this useless death. He donated his wife's vascular organs and tissue, allowing life to flow into another.

Surprisingly, once the decision was made Nancy's husband began to realize that this gift of life helped the healing. Not that day, but in the weeks to come. The coordinators have seen it over and over again. This selfless gift returned the favor. Again and again donor families have stated how they felt their love one continued to live through the art of donating. The pain of loss was comforted through the grace of giving.

Nancy did leave a legacy, more than she knew. Her time on earth may have been short, but due to her gift many others extended their lives. How often are unexpected gifts given that leave such an impact as life? She knew at an early age the importance of offering her best. Little did she realize that the end of her life would be the start for many others.

You know, Carol, with every experience I am blessed to witness such grace. A husband and wife ended their relationship very early, but I know his wife must be smiling. His decision, her gift, saved several children's lives. Nancy left a legacy even greater than her vision imagined.

Goodnight, my dear friend,
Nina

CHAPTER 2

MIRACLES AND GRACE

Dear Carol,

The continuation of Nancy's story is a legacy of its own. That young lady and her husband will never know how their gift began a domino effect.

After surgery to remove Nancy's vascular organs and tissue for donation, her husband returned to the empty home. Little did he contemplate that her unconditional gift to several people across the country was the beginning of new lives for those who feared death at their doorsteps. One cannot imagine the thoughts that raced through his head. Where is my darling now? In a few days the funeral would take place and all that would be left were his memories of

13

her. Her flair that she offered to their home, her zeal for life, could this sustain him? He wondered if he could survive this horrific trauma.

Nancy's husband did not realize the story had a continuation. Nancy's tissue was donated to a two-year-old girl. I was the procurement coordinator. My peer, Margaret, and I were to fly to New York City and bring this vital tissue to surgery to save the small child. Nancy's six-antigen tissue was a perfect match for this young one. Ironically, the north and south came together to save a life. There is always that underlying humor about the dissension between the northern and southern states. But the act of giving transcends all of that history.

So the two-person team, Margaret and myself, made all the necessary arrangements to head to New York City, New York, in the coldest days of winter. Our commercial flight would arrive quickly enough to reach the Manhattan base hospital of Sloan-Kettering. This selfless gift from the teacher who wanted to share her talents with her small little students reached beyond the boundaries of even her own expectations.

As Margaret and I rested quietly on the flight over, we closed our eyes attempting to restore our weary bodies from the long, arduous hours of the previous day's surgery. The amount of energy and alertness that is required from the moment a patient is declared brain dead until the completion of the removal of all vascular organs in surgery can be great.

It is always a double-edge sword, death and life. As a coordinator you have a depth of respect and honoring for the family that has just lost their loved one. This compassion and the importance of the ability to empathize with family members during their horrific grief can't be measured. At the same time that you are the bringer of good news to the desperate family members of another, it could be that a donation will not arrive in time to save a life.

As procurement coordinators, emotions range from grief to praise, which is most understandable. Life

15

persists on one side of the hall while death paid its visit on the opposite side. The transplant team of surgeons and nurses perform the surgical procedures. Great honor and respect go the donor and the family, the heroes in the art of giving. Time and time again I practically felt blessed to witness the love through this giving, especially when the wound was so deep.

Prior to departure, Margaret and I prepared for the trip to New York having the knowledge that we would have plenty of time to prepare for the surgery. However, such was not the case.

The story took place prior to 9-11, and I am not certain the events would have occurred today. In any event, the amount of trust, giving, and believing in the sustenance of life never rung out so true as did in this story.

Almost half way to New York, the pilot announced that the plane was going to be diverted to a nearby state. The weather in New York was too unstable for planes to land.

This could not happen, we needed to be in surgery by six in the evening and there was no way we could contact the hospital to notify them. A small two-year-old was depending us. I immediately called the airline steward and told her about the tissue we were carrying onboard. There we sat with our small red and white igloo container between our feet.

The look in my eyes must have alerted her to the urgency. She told us to wait and she would inform the pilot to the necessity of our arrival in New York. After what seemed like hours because the time passed so slowly, she finally returned to our seat.

She informed us that the pilot had been given special consent to bring the plane into Kennedy Airport because LaGuardia was completely closed to air traffic due to the winds and rain. No one on that plane knew we would arrive in New York because of the gift of someone dying and offering another chance of life to another. This would not happen today, especially after 9-11.

But on that day, the airline steward, the pilot, and even New York Kennedy believed us. Surely, something greater than our plea for assistance was with us; heavenly angels made their presence known that day. All on that plane would indeed reach their destination of New York, and a small child would receive her organ tissue that day.

Margaret and I took a deep breath and thanked our heavenly Father for interceding in that moment. Little did we know the adventure had just begun.

Once we landed it was 5pm and we were in Kennedy airport, which meant that we had to travel all the way into the city and across Manhattan. Thankfully, we traveled with our luggage in hand and did not need to wait for the baggage claim.

As we ran through the airport I announced to Margaret, "Do not worry. I am most familiar with Manhattan, so it will be easy to get a taxi." Little did we know that in the midst of the stormy rain and heavy winds there was a transit strike. Brother, what next? We ran to the curb to our dismay, and I wondered what to do. Then, on the side of my eye I noticed a port authority policeman.

"Mister, mister, please help us. We have to be in surgery at 6pm and there is no transportation to get us there in time."

As I gazed down to look at the time, my heart began to race. Were we going to reach this deadline? With a desperate look in my eyes, I stared deeply into his deep, penetrating look. He gave us a quick look over, saw our small plastic container, and then told us to wait one moment. He said he would call a helicopter to bring us to the hospital.

My first thought was, "Oh no. If planes can't fly in this weather, do I really want to take a helicopter?" The winds were blowing so strongly that I could barely stand up straight. It was dark, rain poured, and the winds made for poor visibility. He did not know, but I said a small prayer, "Please, Lord, if the planes can't land do you think it safe for us to go by helicopter?"

It is amazing the thoughts that race through your mind in a stressful situation. This was clearly a demonstration of my faith. The policeman received his call. He looked at us with disappointment and told us that the weather was entirely too dangerous for us to travel via air. Well, I was relieved. He told us not to worry, that a port authority patrol car was on its way and would help us make the appointed time for surgery. At that point all I could see was backed-up car traffic, rain, wet streets, and darkness. I felt the heavy rain pound against my face. The darkness of this winter's cold, wet evening, the car lights reflecting off of the wet paved streets made for a gloomy night. The tension mounted as the deadline neared.

In fewer than two minutes the patrol car arrived and the policeman opened the car door. He said, "Buckle up, ladies, you're in for a ride." We positioned ourselves securely and what came next can hardly be expressed.

The patrolman turned the car around. We sat securely in the back seat. The policeman had his radio on and was communicating with the port authority. As we anticipated our arrival time he sped down the wet, slippery streets faster than we could imagine possible. The car made its way in and out of traffic. We could not believe our eyes. Margaret and I held tightly to the metal bars separating the driver from us. Then, before we knew it, we were at the Lincoln Tunnel and, to our surprise, even though the port authority had closed the tunnel, we were allowed to swiftly race to our destination—Manhattan. Tears began to roll down our eyes. Only heaven could have made this happen. We went through the Lincoln Tunnel without a single car in our way. As the tears flowed down our cheeks all we could say was, "No one will believe this." The act of giving from a schoolteacher and her husband, small words like *thank you* seem embarrassingly inadequate. The responses of the steward, the airline, the airport police, the patrolman and the port authority—what heroes: this memory never forgotten. It was beyond explanation. Tears poured from our eyes as we praised New York City.

We raced through the tunnel; the tunnel had never looked as bright as it did that night. The patrolman sped on as if he were riding a lightning bolt.

The excitement was not yet at the apex. Next came the navigation through the dark, slippery, wet streets of Manhattan to reach Sloan Kettering Hospital. Then, before we knew it, the car drove on sidewalks, in and out of traffic and even in the wrong direction for a short block. We kept repeating, "No one will ever believe this story."

Finally, we reached the hospital with five minutes to spare. We could hardly fathom that after all that—the airplane landing at 5pm—we still made it on time. The police had arranged for someone to meet us at the front entrance and take us to our final destination.

As she departed the car I told her I needed to obtain the man's name. The Port Authority Policeman opened my door, Margaret grabbed the container and ran up the stairs to the surgery unit. My only words, "Thank you so much. You have just helped save a child's life." I asked his name. He was Patrolman Gonzalez. I shook his hand and thanked him profusely.

He responded, "No worries, lady, it is all in a day's job."'

That statement resonated over and over in my brain, "a day's job." Amazing, but what was more remarkable was that we could not announce this to the world. Several decades have passed since this incident, and although we could not publically acknowledge the response of the commercial airline, the airport authority, the port authority, and the excellent navigation of the patrol car that unforgettable evening on a cold, wet, and windy winter night when New York City was having a transit strike. After 9-11 events could not have happened in this order. That evening the element of trust and giving reached an all-time level of excellence. The world witnessed the response of New York City after 9-11, but what about all those times that we can't make known to the mayor of this dynamic city how his professionals galvanized heroic deeds in critical moments of crisis?

Thankfully, because of Nancy's husband's ability to give, that young child is alive today, and little does she know what effort was given to keep her alive. Only the celestial realms and the grace of that realm witnessed the true heroism of such momentous day.

Carol, once again, I am most appreciative to be able to share a most meaningful experience.

Nina

Chapter 3

God Given Insight Through Music: How the Message Can Be Missed

Dear Carol,

It was a clear November day in Philadelphia. My husband, Frank, and I had flown there just to see Martha Argerich perform at the Kimmel Concert Hall. Her repertoire that afternoon included Sibelius's *Pobjola's Daughter*, Op. 49, Ravel's Piano Concerto in C Minor, and Prokofiev's Symphony No. 6 in E Flat Minor, Op. 111. Soon after her performance began, Ms. Argerich's passion and command of the piano keys struck me to my core. Her interpretation of Prokofiev moved me deeply and brought me to tears. And for some reason––I am still uncertain exactly why––the words wanted to flow; all I wanted to do was write.

When the concert hall lights glowed to signal intermission, I announced to Frank that I had to get paper and something to write with. He thought me silly, but I insisted. I hurried to the gift shop and purchased my pad and pen. Then I returned quickly to my seat. The lights dimmed, the eager listeners began to quiet themselves, and everyone prepared for the next piece. I did not yet begin to write,

I was ready to witness again this lady becoming one with her piano, completely unaware of her surroundings. Maestro Charles Dutoit conducted the orchestra––as well as Ms. Argerich––on this remarkable evening. The two exchanged a few words before they began, and you could see how much he enjoyed being playful with her. She pretended not to be amused. I waited patiently with my pad and pen ready.

I had read rave reviews about Martha Argerich. She was greatly admired by other classical pianists, and although I was not a trained musician, her technique and her relationship with her instrument inspired a passion in me to perform in my own way: to write.

By telling this story, I wish to express my gratitude to Ms. Argerich for the gift her performance offered me that afternoon. Her oneness with the piano, the musical score, and the orchestra invited my creative muse to reappear at the most unusual time. But isn't that so often the case? The strength of my impulse to write that day unnerved my being.

After the lights dimmed and Ms. Argerich resumed her performance, my hand swirled rapidly across the pages of the small notepad. Its cover had musical notes, and each page was about the size of an index card. As I wrote, the darkness prevented me from seeing what words flowed from my pen and onto the paper.

When the performance ended I requested that we return the following night to witness her once again. Frank wondered why, but being the ever-gracious man he was, simply stated that he would attempt to purchase two tickets for her next performance.

So we returned to the concert hall to see another enthralling performance. My appreciation grew as I tentatively listened and then completely lost myself to the presence of Ms. Argerich and the orchestration. Once again, my hand danced across empty lines, filling them with words.

Afterward, we walked to dinner, and to our surprise, there in front of us was Maestro Dutoit walking briskly along the paved street. Excitedly, Frank introduced us to this world-renowned conductor. Both men became engaged in a critique of the night's performance. Frank was definitely in all his glory, as nothing gave him such pleasure as discussing the music, the performance, and the musicians. Maestro Dutoit was very pleasant, but it was clear he was ready to depart for his next appointment that evening; rarely do artists retire early after a concert. We parted ways, and each man carried with him his own interpretation of this exchange of musical orchestration.

Frank had been trained as a classical pianist from the age of three, and music was his first love. He was energized by Ms. Argerich's performance, and he stated that he had always wanted to see her play in person. His eyes were vibrant with life as he acknowledged her great skill in musical piano orchestration.

Once we returned home, I put away my notebook without looking at it. We were so alive with our remembrances of the performance, complemented by a fine dining experience of epicurean wonder, that I completely forgot to read what I had scribbled in the dark concert hall.

And so life continued as usual––or at least I thought it would.

Two weeks later, I traveled to Zurich, Switzerland, for a meeting. Upon my return we were supposed to travel to St. Maarten for a Thanksgiving vacation of relaxation and sun. But that trip was never to transpire. Frank died unexpectedly the morning I was heading home from Switzerland.

For the next several years, the music stopped. It was so painful to attend concerts. His presence was always there, and I missed his critiques, our post-performance conversations, and how much he enjoyed sharing his knowledge with me. When we returned home he would play the selections from the night's performance over and over again as his fingers danced across the piano. He studied the musical scores for hours. Although my civic duties required that I continue attending performances, my heart ached with each musical note I heard. I never allowed anyone to know about this piercing of my heart that occurred with every performance.

Several years later, my daughter came across that little notebook and read what I had written. There was an ongoing joke in our family that I had enough notepads to create my own stationery store, but this notepad stood out because it was dated prior to Frank's departure. Once I obtained the book and began to read, the words stung my heart. Sharing what I wrote in its entirety is unnecessary, but here is the heart of the gifted message offered that November afternoon, brought forth by Martha Argerich.

"I never thought you would be the first to leave. I never thought you would leave me here all alone. Why? Oh, why have you gone? The days left with your memories all alone, sad and lonely. Why? Oh, why have you gone?"

I was shocked. I had written these words during Ms. Argerich's piano performance, and her passion, her interpretation of the composer's music, had resonated so deeply within my soul that day that something outside of myself reached inside to inform me of what was to come. Yet I did not open the notepad to reread what I had scribed. My muse was attempting to inform me of what lay ahead, yet I refused to heed the call.

What was that all about? Could it have been that on some unconscious level I feared reading those informative words? I wonder how many other performances attempt to convey messages to the listeners?

Now, many years later, I wish to acknowledge Martha Argerich's musical interpretation that day. What is expressed between the keys of a keyboard? Where is the luminal space between music and performance? In my life, I have come to enjoy numerous musical genres. Each one has left open the invitation to step beyond my level of reality and dance in another special arena often unknown to me.

As painful as this memory I have shared continues to be, it reminds me that music and death are dear companions. They coexist to help us recall and to rekindle memories. Death and music are closely united, making tomorrow possible.

Ms. Argerich, after learning about her own journey contending with cancer, I wonder if Frank felt the connection to her on another level. He was a classical pianist, and he was a twelve-year cancer survivor. Unknowingly, they both shared something very special. And both Martha and Frank expressed a desire to live through their music; their fingers gave way to a deeply buried passion within.

It is in gratitude that I thank both Martha Argerich and Frank for allowing me to have, yet again, another special connection to the power of music.

Carol, now you can understand how music causes me to listen even more carefully than years gone by. Even today, when the grandchildren's musical toys begin playing without anyone being close by we say, "That's Poppee letting us know he is still around." My family continues to love him ever so deeply to this day. God gave us special years with him, and we are truly appreciative for those times.

Until my next letter, blessings, dear friend.

Nina

CHAPTER 4

THE FULFILLMENT OF THE MESSAGE

Dear Carol,

The night prior to my return to the United States, Frank attended a performance of Brahms's Requiem. The program lay on his nightstand, a reminder that death is always closer than we know.

I learned afterward that he was concerned about time and so had hurriedly run up the stairs so as not to enter the concert hall late. He had enjoyed the performance, but then he stated that he wasn't feeling very well. So why didn't he go to a hospital? I will never have this answer.

Knowing him, I am certain he reviewed the program carefully upon his return home. He enjoyed revisiting the score after each concert.

I can imagine that he reread the words carefully, words that Brahms had translated from a Lutheran Bible. It had been a time of grief in Brahms' life.

I recall this particular verse from the libretto:

"Death is swallowed up in victory. O death, where is thy sting? O grave, where is thy glory?" J. Brahams.

Johannes Brahms' libretto has offered a comfort to many individuals who have grieved over the loss of a love. The creation of his Requiem not only helped heal his own grief, but it has aided many of those who have listened to it since. Did it comfort him during his tragedies? Was it meant to comfort me? As I reread the program, death and music once again performed together.

Carol, is death closer to us than life? Do we walk side by side awaiting its invitation? I know we are here to live, to live abundant and full lives. What else are we here to learn? If death walks so closely to us, is that the gift? To live, to love, to embrace. To see with four eyes, hear with four ears, and smell every fragrance known to humanity? I wonder what we must miss every day. How much laughter have we let slip through our fingertips, never to regain?

Carol, now it is I who must reflect.

Nina

CHAPTER 5

THE ANGEL

Dear Carol,

There have been so many personal stories about Hurricane Katrina, mostly negative. The world of news reporting seems to thrive on featuring the negative aspects of humanity––perhaps the thinking is that negativity will capture more viewers. Take Hurricane Katrina as an example. In the days following the initial impact of the storm, the media was filled with stories documenting the tragedies and devastations that occurred, but there were just as many positive stories available to highlight the good of humanity. Why was the news focused so strongly on the dark side of people during those horrific post-Katrina days? As the long journey toward recovery began, many heroic stories awaited a voice to share them with the world. Survivors eagerly wished to express their disjointed memories of this horrific event. Sharing their personal experiences in this epic tale provided the bandage to begin the healing process.

In the crazy, mixed-up world in which we live, we face choices every day. More often than not, if we find ourselves in traumatic situations we will react in the moment and hope our quick decisions will serve us well in the future. I feel privileged to describe a moment like this, when I had to place my fate in the hands of a complete stranger and trust that my discernment would serve me properly. In an instant I had to stare into the unknown eyes and desperately hope he spoke the truth.

In hindsight, I am uncertain of what I was thinking, but I had decided to stay in New Orleans during Katrina. The terrible heat of August, no electricity, no water, no services of any kind that would help sustain an individual was experienced by all who remained. Being a resident of Louisiana, I experienced many hurricanes as a child, and I knew the precautionary steps. I received several calls from friends telling me I was crazy to stay. The force of this storm was nothing to take lightly, they warned. The last call came from my friend Herma Edwards, who lived in New Orleans East. It was midnight, August 29, 2005, and her exact words were, "Girl, you need to get out of there."

At that time in my life, I was living alone. I thought that if I stayed I could serve my community and preserve the Children's Bureau. Witnessing the panic coming from the storms harnessed my psyche in the way that would never be erased. I was engulfed by the visuals of the hurricane and stunned emotionally by the powerful and energetic forces of nature. Staring out of the window, I wondered, "Will the horrors of Katrina ever cease?" The winds engulfed the skyline. The sky darkened as the rains pounded over the earth. The sheer force of these sounds demanded a captive audience. Mother Nature was speaking and commanded our attention; she would not be taken lightly. And so New Orleans stood lifeless as Katrina made her presence known.

Tuesday morning, August 30, finally arrived, and the air cleared from the night before. The heat and humidity of August pressed down against the city's remains. I thought the city of New Orleans has survived. But little did I know the totality of its destructive forces. The remnants made their presence known: no electricity, no water, no telephone, no cell communication. Radio towers had been destroyed throughout Orleans and Jefferson Parishes. The city was unprepared for this kind of devastation.

Then came a voice from the hallway: "The city is flooding, and you have fifteen minutes to vacate this building and leave the city." Only three people remained in our building: William Oliver, the president of ATT; Richard Zachlag, the president and owner of Acadian Ambulance; and me. They were quickly removed from the devastation via police security services. It was not until later, as we all shared our stories, that they came to know I had remained in the building as well.

Immediately after the city's population began vacating, the city became flooded with a new, more lethal danger: uninvited intruders. They came to rob the unguarded property left behind by those who had fled. But where did they think the stolen goods would find a home? The bowl that formed the landscape of New Orleans was being filled with water, and only rooftops provided any kind of decoration to the environment.

The security guard in the building where I resided, Dave Hymel, explained to me that the city would soon fill with twenty feet of water and that everyone must leave New Orleans as soon as possible. I could not believe my ears. The sun was shining brightly, there was no apparent rain, and to my observation we had already survived the worst. But the worst was still to come! I was tired at that point because it had already been a two-day ordeal considering all the preparation and then listening to the news until all communication ceased.

As a southern lady, my first thought was that I needed to wear a dress, get my wallet, and a throw a few items into an overnight bag. And wouldn't you know, I had just finished unpacking my emergency bag, thinking all was clear and the worst thing left to get through was waiting patiently for the electricity to be restored. And now who knew where I would spend the coming night? I was simply told to head east.

So I jumped into my car, pulled out of the garage, and promptly drove toward Canal Street. To my surprise, people were everywhere wandering through the streets. I witnessed individuals breaking glass windows and going into closed buildings. I noticed the water rising in the streets, and I sensed the turmoil and horrific reactions from the strangers around me. This was not good. A feeling of danger visited my bones. People were removing large items from department stores. Where did they think they would go with them? Everything was destroyed!

To say I was apprehensive is an understatement. The horrific winds and rains of the storms had not caused me as much fear as I was feeling at that moment. People moved frantically yelling. It was frightening. I wanted out of the scene as quickly as possible. I had never witnessed anything like it before. Why were they acting this way? Why destroy anything that survived? Wasn't there enough destruction already? Couldn't we come together like the people of New York City had after 9-11? What was happening?

I knew I had to turn around and remove myself from Canal Street immediately. Instead of helping the homeless, strangers were destroying the property that nature left unharmed. Anger and aggression reared their ugly heads. The worst side of humanity appeared, showing a horrible, gloomy face.

As I reversed the car and turned around, a thousand thoughts raced through my mind. Why were people breaking windows? Stealing? These were not the visitors that my city needed. As I drove the car down Poydras Street, the water continued rising and the malignant excitement of the survivors escalated. It was not comforting at all.

What happened next is still unclear. I turned from Canal and made a side trip up Poydras Street, eventually finding myself heading up the onramp taking me toward New Orleans East, as per the instructions from my building's security guard. I had to drive in the middle of the two-lane road, as that was the higher ground. I was in a very low sport car and the rising water kept coming. As I traveled up the ramp to get on I-10 heading east, my car passed the first state trooper I had seen. He did not warn me to stop. And so, with a sigh of relief, I thought I was safe. Then a second state trooper allowed me to continue on my journey. I was beginning to feel optimistic. There were no other vehicles traveling this highway, but I did not give it a second thought; everyone had left the city and only a few individuals, for their own personal reasons, had remained behind.

Once I reached the third state trooper, he flagged his arms. I stopped the car, and he looked at me strangely. "Where do you think you are going?" the state trooper emphatically asked.

"I am going to New Orleans East," I replied with the positive reassurance that I was taking the proper way out of New Orleans.

"Lady, if you keep going this direction, you will drive directly into the canal," he said with no trace of humor. "New Orleans East has been totally devastated."

"Mister, what should I do?" I asked, responding with a sign of anxiousness.

His stressed response was, "Lady, I do not care what you do. Just get out of here."

I-10 East was a four–lane, one-direction road departing from downtown New Orleans and leading directly toward New Orleans East and Slidell, and then continuing toward the Mississippi Gulf Coast. I now felt my anxiety rising. So I asked if it was all right to travel in the opposite direction.

His emphatic response: "Lady, I do not care what you do, just get out of here."

I was completely overwhelmed and stressed. I had not slept for two days. I did not know where to go or which direction to head. I later learned from the state police that all towers were down and communication was almost nonexistent. So the state trooper had given me the best answer he could. After all, he did not have any answers, as all communication was destroyed.

I turned the car around, but this time I gazed from the overpass and all I could see was water nestling comfortably against the edges of rooflines. Once again I was shaken to my core. My city was under water. Just the remnants of rooftops peeked above the stillness of resting water, as if it had found a new home.

I drove the car hurriedly back to the city, but each exit off the ramp proved futile, as water greeted the upper concrete ramp levels. I could feel my face becoming flushed with worry and anxiousness. After attempting three exit ramps, I drove and parked on the overhead pass immediately opposite the Super Dome. I stopped the car and saw a few stragglers walking along the concrete overpass that linked I-10 east and west sections. It was high noon, and I recall the heat beating down with no reprieve. The sun felt closer to earth than it should have been, its penetrating rays of heat baked the hard concrete. The penetrating heat jumped off the payment reaching for the faces of those individuals standing still, crying for help. The blistering sun burned from above and from below. It was hot, humid, and absent of any breeze. Everyone had the same question: What do we do now? We were stranded.

The heat of August in New Orleans is relentless and exacerbated by humidity. You would not wish the hot days of August following a tropical storm on your worst enemy. The air didn't move, and the absence of life only added to the anxiety.

I focused on the deafening noise of military helicopters landing at the Superdome. I will never forget that sound. It penetrated my ears and I felt the vibrations throughout my body. I was reminded of combat scenes from movies I had seen. I saw people around me crying for water, and I wondered, "What's next?"

Tremendous fear gripped my inner being. I was afraid. People screamed for help. "Help!" "Help!" "Help me, please!" Between the heat, the noise from the helicopters, and the cries of the people, it all became quite surreal. My mind raced to resolve the nightmare. The helicopters dropped off soldiers who would try to bring some semblance of order to the tired and weary individuals who had spent time sheltered in the New Orleans Superdome. The heat pounded down on those standing outside, witnessing the cries of folks streaming out from the Superdome's shelter. A very weary looking lady offered me her wet towel so I could moisten my face. I received her gesture as a sign of kindness, but the second the towel touched my face I understood it was not kindness but cruelty—the towel burned my skin immediately. Why did she do this? What was the point? Did she think I would blind myself and she would take my car and whatever meager possessions I had that day? I was relieved that I had not placed the damaging chemical towel on my eyes.

To add to the insult of the situation, my skin now burned. And along with the heat rising from the hot summer concrete and the penetrating sun, it only added to an already painful sensation. Scars remain on my cheeks to this day as a reminder.

My fear was suddenly greater than it had been at any point yet. As the night drew near and the day concluded, would my life come to conclusion as well? There I stood, a single woman in a long, black cotton dress, a two-door sports car, and I was trapped. This was one time in my life I regretted having that old white car. The thoughts racing through my mind were variations of how this story would end. Each face I gazed upon that solemn day wore the same expression: "is this how my life will end?" etched in concrete, lifeless, hot, faces void of sensitivity. That day the sun seemed too close, and not even the birds had remained in the city after the winds of Katrina passed and left their mark.

Outgoing cellular calls were impossible, but after about thirty minutes of being on the overpass I received an incoming call from one of the social workers, Gaspard Bongovania. He had taken a vacation to New York to attend a toy fair, a trip fitting of him, as Gaspard always had the cheerfulness and kindness of a child spirit. He was calling to say he could not get back to New Orleans for work. I begged him to hold on as I retrieved a telephone number for a friend in Houston, Texas. As bizarre as this might sound, I pleaded with him to call my friend and ask him to arrange for a helicopter to pick me up. The bizarreness of my wish or its extravagant cost were nowhere in my mind. I couldn't have cared less. All I was thinking was that I would be dead if I did not get out of that scenario before the day faded into evening. Can you imagine asking someone to send you a helicopter? I saw helicopters landing, so I knew my request was at least feasible.

But I was not thinking properly. Who could get a helicopter? Once I was off the phone, a young man came up to me and said, "You must be someone important." I smiled and replied, "No, I'm no one. I just want out of this situation." At least twelve people had witnessed the woman giving me the toxic towel and the result of my acceptance. Now I waited patiently, with burned, reddened flesh on my checks and eyes burning from the torrid heat pounding against the pavement. I stood alone, and I contemplated how it would all end.

The response seemed to take forever, but finally, after about forty minutes, Gaspar called back. He said no aircraft could come within a thousand miles of New Orleans, with the exception of the military aircraft. My heart sank to my knees, and I knew it would be the last night of my life. I thanked Gaspard and asked him to try to keep in touch.

I stood by my car and asked God for help. The helicopters were still landing, still dropping off soldiers. The people coming out of the dome continued to scream for water and assistance. My eyes gazed at this scene. I wondered again how this could happen in this day and age. We are America, a strong nation. We are not a third-world country. What about all of those helpless people in the dome, with the heat, with no air-conditioning, with no water? One could surely appreciate their level of stress. What thoughts were going through their minds? I could only imagine the fear that surrounded them.

My eyes couldn't stray from those people on the other side of the overpass. Until you are confronted with tragedy, you never know how you will respond. My heart was so heavy with the pain of hearing and witnessing the cries coming from the men, women, and children heading out into the light of day for fresh air. Then I heard a deep voice speaking next to me. I turned around and gazed upon a very tall, broad-shouldered man. His back was to the sun, so his facial features were in shadow. At that moment, all I could make out was his body shape, that he was a muscular, African-American man. He looked into my eyes as he said, "Lady, if you give me a ride, I will get you out of this city."

With my cheeks still burning from my last experience of trust in this situation, I looked directly back into his eyes and asked, "Are you a good man?"

Without hesitation, he responded, "I am a very good man."

Acting on impulse, I instantly replied, "Let's go."

The minute I opened the trunk of my car to place his duffle bag safely inside, people began running toward us. The young man who had previously commented on my importance begged to come along, but I apologized that the vehicle only held two people. My new passenger looked forcibly into my eyes and said, "Let's go."

I wanted to give the young man a ride. I saw the fear and sadness in his eyes, and it pained my heart. But the new stranger insisted, "He can't fit in the car." My heart felt the disappointment deeply, and I apologized to the young man, telling him how sorry I was. I knew not to linger. The night would soon arrive and I had gotten what I prayed for: a way to escape this frightening scene. So I took a deep breath and started the car. And I prayed one more time: *Dearest Heavenly Father, let me live to see another day, if it is your will.* And the same sentence raced repeatedly through my mind: "I do believe in miracles! I do believe in miracles!"

Then it dawned on me: how could we get off this ramp if water is all around us? But I just knew from the look in his eyes that he had a plan, and this was our only opportunity. He knew it as well. There was no time to waste. We needed to move.

I listened to his instructions as he guided me safely off the overpass and back down onto the streets. To this day, I do not recall how he guided me off the overpass. I drove, but he knew the city better than I did at that point so he was in charge. We continued driving until we arrived at the West Bank Mississippi River Bridge. I believe we were the last moving vehicle allowed to travel over that bridge before all traffic was stopped. The only motor vehicle I witnessed as we crossed was a huge black Hummer also traveling away from the devastated city.

As we moved away from scenes that were burned into my mind, the first smile I had in three days crossed my face. As I looked over at the passenger in my car, I called him my angel. I continued calling him my angel over and over again. I was so appreciative that he had come to my aid, that he had the wisdom and foresight to approach me. Where did he come from? It really did not matter. All that mattered was that he arrived before the sun withdrew its radiance from the city.

As we meandered along the windy old Louisiana roads, attempting to head west, our first destination became Baton Rouge. Under normal circumstances it would have taken about an hour to drive fifty miles, but with the interstate closed between New Orleans and Baton Rouge we had to travel back roads. Even so, it should not have taken as long as it did, but trees had fallen across the roads and long lines of local traffic leaving the rural coastal areas clogged the route. It became a six-hour journey.

But the long, arduous drive provided a gift: we had ample time to share stories. As we journeyed along the desolate roads my angel told me he had saved twenty lives that day, placing them on rooftops in anticipation of the arrival of recovery teams. He also shared that his family––his wife and his mother–– had lost everything, and it would be up to him to explain that nothing remained. His journey was much longer than mine. I witnessed the emptiness in his eyes. He was exhausted.

I listened intently to his story. After several hours, though, I realized we did not know each other's names. All I knew was that he was my saving angel. He soon told me his name was Mr. Gibson, and that he worked for an offshore oil company.

As our journey continued, Mr. Gibson looked at me and stated in his quiet, soft manner, "You keep speaking of angels, but I believe in dragons."

Oh, no, I thought. I don't know this man, and here we are on a long country road, both of us having experienced acute trauma, and now he informs me that he believes in dragons. Oh, boy. What next?

I had studied mythology in the past, and what I had learned came to mind suddenly. I knew there were both good and bad dragons, so I settled down and replied, "Mr. Gibson, do you know that the Chinese believe in dragons as guides and protectors? That's you, a guide and protector and leader. So, thank you, Mr. Gibson, for honoring those qualities. You are truly a special spirit. You have saved twenty people today. Thank you, and bless you."

Mr. Gibson remained silent as we traveled down that lonely road. Secretly, I hoped he understood that I meant what I said. We finally made it to Baton Rouge many hours later. As we pulled into a service station we witnessed panic everywhere. People were lined up to fill their cars and large containers with gasoline. People were stocking up on water and food supplies. Although the hurricane was over, people were unsure about where to find housing or how they would meet their basic needs. The surreal scene etched itself into my memory forever.

Now that we were stopped, I suggested Mr. Gibson should try to reach his family. He told me his family members had traveled to Monroe, Louisiana. He added he had a son attending the University of Louisiana in Lafayette, and he would be happy if I could bring him to the campus. I agreed, so we traveled in that direction. I apologized for not bringing him directly to Monroe, but I explained that I needed to stay on I-10 to find lodging. He completely understood.

Traveling once again down the long highway, we continued sharing stories. When we reached Lafayette——the place where our journey together ended——I got out of the car and gave him a sincere hug of love and gratitude. My parting words were, "Just think, Mr. Gibson, you saved twenty lives today."

"No, little lady, I saved twenty-one." His response was very serious, and I wondered, "How could I have been so remiss in my counting as to not include myself?"

"Oh, Mr. Gibson," I replied shamefully, "you are so right. Forgive me."

As I drove away, I thanked God that this man had entered my life, knowing that he had saved me from the nightmare of spending the night on the bridge. I thanked Mr. Gibson too, and wished him blessings wherever his path would take him. I saw my life pass in front of me, and I thanked my angels. I thanked life for allowing me to see another day. Yes, my heart was filled with appreciation. I also reflected on the fact that Mr. Gibson still had to inform his family that they had lost their homes and that life would never be the same for any of them. All physical memories vanished. It was a true death of another form.

The image of Mr. Gibson reflected in my rearview mirror lingered in my mind for hours. I knew he had forever left an imprint upon my heart. He had saved my life. The word *grateful* seemed like such an empty, trival expression compared to the appreciation I felt. As I traveled down the long, lonely road that night, looking for a place to rest, visions of the day kept circling through my mind.

The entire experience kept me company that long night, and I knew the horrors of the day would occupy my mind for a long time to come. I continued on, driving without knowing where I would stop to rest my head for the evening.

In just those few hours when our paths had crossed, I understood clearly that Mr. Gibson was, indeed, a good man and even perhaps an angel. And as much as I see the story in terms of my having taken a chance on him, this stranger had also been willing to take a chance on me. There were no reservations about color or creed, we were just strangers on common ground looking for safety. Wouldn't it be great if we could see others through their eyes only?

Mr. Gibson and I shared so many stories on that long journey. I spoke of angels almost the entire time, and he spoke briefly of dragons. As a mythologist, I knew there were dark dragons, but I chose to see only the light in Mr. Gibson's intentions. As the hours passed, I knew he was an angel sent to remove me safely from the city. Mr.Gibson had eventually given me his email address so we could stay in touch. When communications were finally restored quite sometime after Katrina I made many attempts to communicate with Mr. Gibson, but to no avail. Why do you think that might be? For that day and forever, I will remember Mr. Gibson, his eyes, and his stature as larger than life. I have prayed many times for his health and the restoration of his family.

During the months following the ordeal I must have told that story hundreds of times. Doing so was my small way of honoring Mr. Gibson. His eyes had spoken truth and sincerity, and so, with an instant to decide, I had chosen trust. Even in the darkest hours of tragedy, goodness waits for acknowledgement.

Carol, I will never forget the deep, penetrating look in Mr. Gibson's eyes. My life was in his hands. We both knew we needed to remove ourselves from that scene and there was no time to discuss it. As I looked into his eyes, I saw goodness. I knew he was a man of integrity, and I trusted him. Heaven knows I have thanked his presence more times than I can number. He reassured me the world was still a wonderful place.

Carol, I close this letter with true gratitude that Mr. Gibson stepped into my life that day. I have never been the same.

Nina

CHAPTER 6

THE DRIVE OF THE SPIRIT

Dear Carol,

The day began as they all do here in the Crescent City of New Orleans: the fresh morning breeze reminded walkers of a river flowing nearby. The melody of a happy sparrow let everyone know it was time to greet the new day. Fresh morning sunshine filtered between the buildings and shared the brilliant radiance with all who wished to greet the sun. Flavorful aromas seeped up from the cracks in the pavement and, as a reminder of yesterday's activities, remnants of nature made their way through the concrete streets and paved sidewalks.

Early morning is especially pleasant in the town of New Orleans, as the sun glistening breaks slowly over the river. As I walked to work on that particular morning, I noticed the same young man sitting on a curb that I had seen many times before. We smiled at one another every day without sharing a word. He was exceptional in stature, appearing to be over six feet tall with a slender body and the most radiant face. His complexion was one to admire, and he exuded a powerful inner glow. My curious nature finally led me to wonder, "How does this gentleman occupy his day?"

So I decided that if I wanted to learn more about this individual who seemed to never move from this curb, I would need to speak with him.

"Hello, sir. What is your name?" I inquired.

"Randal Scott," he answered. He asked in return, "What is your name?"

"My name is Nina. I am pleased to meet you."

We exchanged a few more words, and then I hurriedly left to continue on with my daily responsibilities.

A few weeks later I finally had the courage to ask what he did all day. He informed me that he did not have a job. He lived in a homeless shelter, but each morning everyone had to leave for the day. They could return to the shelter again in the evening. So he spent his day watching the traffic move steadily down the street.

"Well, Mr. Scott, would you like to begin washing my car each week?" I asked.

With hesitance, he answered, "Sure. Let me find out if the parking lot attendant will let me use his water. I have a bucket."

"Great," I answered. "Then I will bring my car in the morning and pick it up at lunchtime."

So the very next day, I drove my car to the street corner where Mr. Scott sat, parked the vehicle, and told him I would return for it at noon. When I returned, the car was shiny and clean, and there stood a proud Mr. Scott. Thus began our business relationship.

Once a week he cleaned my car. Eventually he began washing several other cars owned by people who worked in the business offices across the street. Each morning I witnessed him walking to his parking lot area with his empty bucket in hand. My heart was moved to see how he solicited business, and soon many individuals engaged him to keep their vehicles clean. He polished and shined those cars until they shone like new copper pennies.

As Mr. Scott continued with his car washing operation, I noticed that each day, as I passed him on my way to work, he stood taller and smiled more and more. Many months had passed before that smile first came forward. I always admired him, and we exchanged a few sentences each day.

One day I was running late for work. I drove into the parking place where he cleaned cars for the day, and as I handed him my keys, I asked if he would please place my car back in the garage when he was finished and hand my keys to the security man in our condo building. For what seemed like an hour, he stared at me. Then he replied, "Sure."

Upon returning from a long, tedious day, my car was securely placed in the appropriate parking spot and the keys had been given to the security guard just as I requested.

Everyone thought I had lost my mind, but there was honor in this man that needed a chance to express itself. It was apparent in the inner glow that shone from his eyes; he wanted another opportunity in life. I knew the two of us had a very special, unspoken understanding.

He often stopped me and asked questions about my work. In return, I inquired about his life. His honesty so struck my heart. He readily admitted that he had made some mistakes in his life, and it was those mistakes that had brought him to where he was today. But the human spirit is far greater than our poor decisions. Thankfully, we have a resilience that walks alongside us through our unhealthy decisions. Then life changed for hundreds of thousands of people. August 29, 2005: Hurricane Katrina struck New Orleans and the surrounding parishes, causing major devastation. I will never forget the aftermath of that disaster, but that story will be saved for later. Everyone in southern Louisiana was affected by the devastation, and I recall one woman pointing out that the hurricane affected much more than just Louisiana. We never realized how much industry and commerce filtered through those Louisiana, Mississippi, and Florida highways. It seemed that life had ceased to exist along the southern coastal region of the United States.

Eventually the winds of Hurricane Katrina caused nearly everyone to vacate the city––even those of us who had remained in place from a sense of duty––and that was how I lost contact with Mr. Scott.

But then one day, a year after the aftermath of Katrina, I saw Mr. Scott on the street once again. I ran to greet him and asked how he had survived the terrible storm.

He appeared slimmer to me, yet he still glowed with that inner optimism.

A twinkle in his eye, he responded, "I am homeless, remember? I know how to survive."

We both laughed at his response and began to catch up on his life. Apparently we now had even more in common, as we had both remained in the city during the hurricane and had many stories to share. What really mattered to both of us seemed to be asking what our lives were about.

He told me that he had since moved out of the Mission and into his own apartment, and he had even purchased a used car. To say the least, I was so thrilled and impressed at his stamina and his desire to continue pressing forward against all odds.

As we spoke, I knew that was the perfect opportunity to learn more about who the real Mr. Scott was. Mr. Scott was born on December 13, 1952, at Charity Hospital in New Orleans. His family consisted of four brothers and two sisters. Both of his parents were deceased. He shared with me that he had left New Orleans for a period of time and moved to Chicago, but he returned in 1979. He told me he had never married, but he had two children, a boy and girl. They were grown, but, at least at that time, he did not have any contact with them.

Mr. Scott openly admitted that he had made some very bad decisions in his life, and it took him time to recover from those choices. Most of his friends were either in jail or deceased. He explained that he had worked hard during his life, delivering groceries, working in pipe yards for the oil field industry, and at other odd jobs that he could find.

When he was younger, he mostly lived with his mother. He had to stop school in seventh grade to help support his family. He told me that his mother kept the family together, and he missed her terribly since she died.

He asked me if I had finished my education, because he saw that I was taking notes as we spoke. I am not certain why, but I asked him where he found peace. He answered, "Through Jesus Christ." He continued by saying that the Mission had given him lessons in the evenings, and that had given him hope for the future.

He told me that he did not have many friends. He enjoyed football, basketball, cars, and music. I laughed when he said, "You know, I am learning to like all types of music: rap, rhythm and blues, jazz. And I especially like the messages of B.B. King. Once upon a time, I did not listen to the words, but I do today."

He told me he had dreams for the future: getting a better car, saving some money, and continuing to adapt to whatever life has in store for him.

My final question was whether he had a message that he would like to give to the world. He answered immediately, "Yes. Learn to adapt to your surroundings."

Then he added, "When I die, I hope to have something to leave behind, something to pass on to anyone who needs a helping hand."

When our talk was coming to an end he asked, "What are you going to do with all that writing?"

"I am going to write your story and place it in a book," I answered.

"A real book?" he asked.

"Yes, and I am even going to place your photo in the book. You will be one of many stories, but you surely will have a prominent place."

Then he stood in front of his car and I took his photo. He said, "Hurry up and finish that book. I want my copy."

Our conversation ended with him stating, "One day I am going to get a better car. Whatever I have that can help someone else they can have. This will be my gift."

Carol, he is a hero in my world. Oh, not the kind that is often recognized, but the resilient glow that resides deep within one's being. Mr. Scott demonstrates the resilience of the human spirit and how its love for life continues in the face of adversity. Love, a small, one-syllable word. I wish there was another word that could describe Mr. Scott. Little does he know how much I respect him for never giving up.

Goodnight, dear Carol, until my next letter. Thank you for always allowing me to share my journeys. As I reflect on these precious stories I remain humble in honor of the heroes of these precious experiences.

Nina

CHAPTER 7

THE IMPORTANCE AND IMPERATIVE OF LOVE

Dear Carol,

I would like to share a story that touched me so deeply. In my years of working as a procurement coordinator for organ donation, all stories pierced my heart in some form or fashion. This one brought to my awareness how one's family can vanish in the blink of an eye. On this particular morning I was faced with witnessing a husband and father having to acknowledge the tragic loss of his wife and only child. He tried to be strong, but how can anyone during such grief? My heart searched for the appropriate words. I prayed, silently begging for the grace to face this situation. Words seemed so empty. The loss of both wife and child, they would never again visit his eyes. Carol, every time I share one of these memories I recall how I hurriedly went home and, on my knees, thanked the Great Divine for protecting my love ones.

That morning was cool and damp, and fog traveled lightly across the pavement as if to share a warning: be careful, traveler, how fast you go. But morning traffic rushed along as usual, everyone hurrying to his or her destination. Most people left home late, waiting until the last minute to depart because something else had called.

This particular weekday morning, a mother and daughter headed toward school and work. Theirs was a typical household. Everyone was in a rush, looking ahead toward the day: mother focused on the challenges that lay ahead, daughter worried about incomplete homework from the night before, and father already on the highway, making his first morning calls. This was an exceptionally cool, damp, foggy day. The visibility was so poor that one could barely see five feet in front of the car. As they drove steadily down the highway, an eighteen-wheeler crossed the medium and hit the unsuspecting car at full force. The impact so devastated the structure of the car one would think it was an accordion.

The driver of the eighteen-wheeler had applied his brakes quickly to prevent rear-ending the car in front of him. The road, wet and slippery from the downpour, sent his rig swaying and sliding across the grassy median and carried it forward into oncoming traffic. In the flash of seconds life for those individuals was changed forever.

The two passengers in the car were instantly crushed. Traffic was halted for hours. State troopers, ambulances, and fire trucks lined the scene. Mother and daughter were rushed to the nearest hospital emergency room, where the trauma specialists were called in to give them full attention. But the outcome was tragic. Both mother and daughter were declared brain dead. The ER staff was shocked. It was not even seven thirty in the morning. What a terrible event to witness and begin the day. Two family members removed from life, and now the saddest part: notifying the husband. The husband and father had to acknowledge the harsh reality that he would never return to his home after work looking into the eyes of his wife and daughter.

After the physician delivered the news that the husband's wife and daughter were declared medically brain dead, I was called in to speak to the father next. My job was to request consent for donations. As always, I prayed prior to speaking to him. What words would I find? How do you comfort a father and husband? I prayed that I would find the appropriate words before entering this space. My heart could not even conceive losing my spouse or my child. I knew the pain of losing a parent at an early age, but that was not the same as the pain he was enduring. Pain has its different markers. Oftentimes grief is more than a human mind can comprehend.

When we met, his first words were, "I never said goodbye."

Oh, could I relate. I never had the opportunity to say goodbye to my mother when I was only seven years of age. That always left an indelible mark on my psyche. I knew the importance of having the chance to wish our loved ones a pleasant day or tell them how much we love them. I learned early in life never to take for granted the people we love will always be there. Life happens, circumstances can alter our plans in the blink of an eye.

He began telling me that he left the house very early and failed to say goodbye to either of them, and now he had lost them both at the same time. My heart anguished for him. His grief seemed unbearable, yet I had the responsibility of asking him to consider giving his wife's and daughter's vascular organs at a time when that seemed incomprehensible.

As I spoke, I looked into his eyes. His intense pain looked back at me. I silently prayed for the proper words to both comfort yet remain professional. I could only imagine what was racing through his mind as he listened carefully to my words. Could they resonate with what I was requesting?

I left him for a while so he could spend time alone peacefully in the hospital room with his loved ones. He bent across the bed and tenderly kissed his daughter's cheeks while the tears flowed from his deeply saddened eyes. He cried passionately while staring at his lifeless wife. "This can't be real," he stated.

As I waited outside the room, the hospital halls bustled with the morning emergencies, doctors, nurses, and all of the ancillary staff unaware that in a small, quiet room a man faced the reality of tremendous loss while at the same time having to make a major critical decision

When I finally returned, he looked deeply into my eyes and said, "If only I could have said goodbye. I will never have an opportunity to express those words ever again," cried the man.

This penetrated to my core. I knew the deep pain of never being able to hold, kiss, or gaze into the eyes of those we love so dearly. Yes, this portion of his pain I knew, but I could only look back with compassion, as no words were appropriate to comfort him at that time.

He took a deep breath and then said, "I have decided to donate all of their organs, with the exception of the heart. I just can't donate their hearts." He muttered in a low tone, "Will you please forgive me for that?"

"Oh my, there is nothing to forgive," I explained. "The greatest act of love is being able to give to another during the most sorrowful times. Please know that even if you decide not to donate any organs at all, that is all right. The very thought that you would even consider offering life to another is gracious. I know you are still stunned."

He told me that he wanted others to live, and he believed that this act and knowing that his family would live on through others would help him heal.

He explained to me that the only reason he could not donate their hearts was because he wanted their hearts to remain with him. He bent down and cried so deeply. My own heart felt such compassion for this man.

We were together for the next many hours as I prepared to call in all the vascular surgeons for the task ahead. Although the hours were long and stressful, I always held on to my memories of how the ones left behind to grieve need a way of making sense of tragedy.

Over and over again, I was impressed that the gift of life––the act of donation––was able to offer donor families a glimpse of healing. Time and time again, as I followed up with the surviving family members, I was informed that their decision had helped with the healing process. This amazed me, yet over and over again, these were the words that I heard from the donors. I couldn't help thinking about the words, "It is in giving that we receive," uttered by St. Frances of Assisi. Such was the case, each and everytime as I listened to the words from the donor families.

At the closure of another chapter in life, the words resonated again and again: *I was never able to say goodbye.* I too experienced that lament when my mother died unexpectedly. I realize that life does not promise us tomorrow, and I understand the value of memories. We are fortunate to share experiences, the good, not so good, the happy, and sad times. Those moments weave together to form the fabric called life. In those hospital corridors I never met anyone who wished to be absent of relationship. Those cold iron beds were filled with patients wishing to spend more time with the people who meant the most to them.

When I entered the surgery with all the vascular teams, I shared this man's story. We never know when such tragedy could knock on our door. As surgery came to completion, everyone in the surgical suite reflected on the importance of the reminder of those last moments when we're walking out of the door. Smile and kiss the ones you love, say goodbye.

Carol, thank you again for allowing me to share the gift life offered me today. Every day there is yet another lesson to place into our little bags of skin. I often reflect on how quickly one forgets those treasured offerings.

Until our next sharing,

Nina

Barry James Cooper, Jr. Esq., Photographer